NATIONAL GEOGRAPHIC

Ladders

YOSEMITE National Park

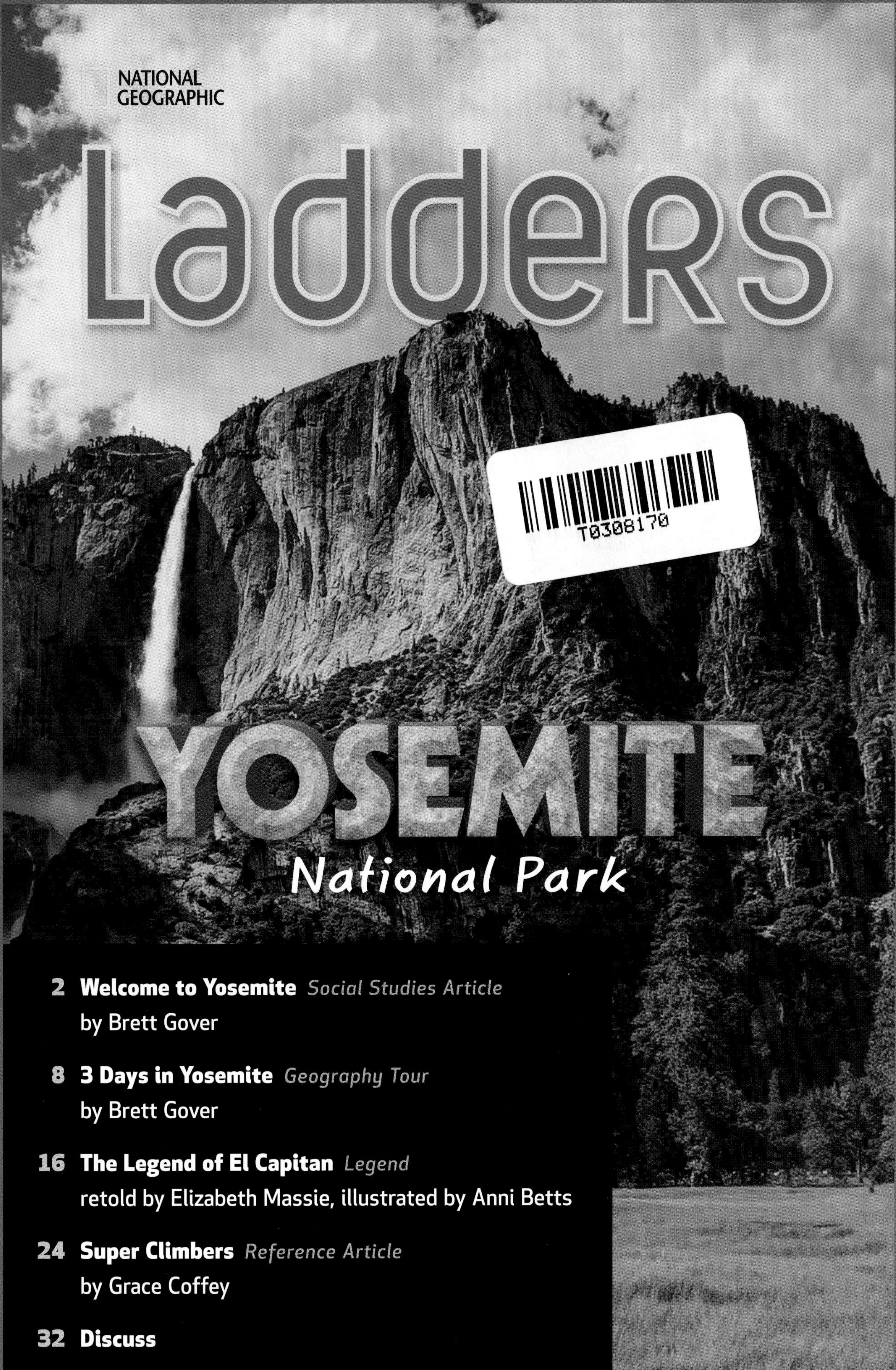

GENRE **Social Studies Article**

Read to find out how Yosemite became a national park.

WELCOME TO YOSEMITE

by Brett Gover

Millions of years ago, nature began shaping a spectacular landscape in what is now eastern California. Racing rivers carved deep valleys on the slopes of a young mountain range we call the Sierra Nevada. **Glaciers**, or slow-moving rivers of ice, formed along the top ridges of the mountain range and crept downward. As the glaciers moved, they plowed away soil and sculpted jagged peaks into rounded mounds.

Glaciers carved the Yosemite Valley from the rocks of the Sierra Nevada.

The glaciers did their most remarkable work in the low valleys between the mountains. Like giant bulldozers, they scraped away huge amounts of rock. Slowly, they made the valleys broader, steeper, and deeper. As the glaciers melted, they left huge piles of rock, sand, and mud that dammed streams and formed lakes. The streams carried more sand and mud, which they deposited behind the dams. The lakes slowly filled with mud and, over many thousands of years, were transformed into green meadows.

When the first humans reached the area, they discovered a land of rocky domes, towering granite walls, plunging waterfalls, broad meadows, and gigantic trees. Today, this scenic land is preserved as Yosemite (yo-SEH-mih-tee) National Park.

PROTECTING YOSEMITE

Native Americans were the first to enter the Yosemite Valley. Historians believe that they have lived in the area for thousands of years. It was not until the mid-1800s that a group of U.S. citizens from a nearby settlement first entered Yosemite Valley. The word quickly spread about this region's unusual features. Soon, more and more people—including miners, settlers, and visitors—started coming to the valley.

One visitor was a young **naturalist** named John Muir. He fell in love with the place, but he worried that people were damaging its natural environment by cutting down the trees, building ranches, and mining for gold. He fought for years to have Yosemite protected as a national park. His wish was finally granted in 1890. The park would forever be a safe **habitat** for the plants and animals of Yosemite's mountain and forest **ecosystems**.

1851

California settlers enter Yosemite Valley and find Miwok Indians living there. The Miwok people still live in the region today.

1890

Thanks to the work of John Muir, the U.S. Congress establishes Yosemite National Park. President Theodore Roosevelt (left) visits the park with John Muir (right).

Today, Yosemite National Park is one of the most popular parks in the national park system. Each year, more than three million people travel to the Sierra Nevada to enjoy Yosemite's natural beauty and observe its mountain wildlife. With all of these tourists enjoying the park's protected land, some parts of Yosemite can become very crowded. But since the park covers nearly 1,200 square miles—an area almost as large as the state of Rhode Island—it's not hard to find wide open spaces, peace, and quiet.

1907

Workers complete a railroad from Merced, California, to Yosemite. This makes it easier for people to travel there. Visitors flock to California to see the park.

1986

Sierra Nevada bighorn sheep are reintroduced to Yosemite. It had been 72 years since one had been seen in the park.

2011

More than 3 million people visit Yosemite. Many take the short hike to the foot of Bridalveil Fall, one of Yosemite Valley's most famous attractions.

This is the famous giant sequoia, the Grizzly Giant. One of the tree's branches measures nearly 7 feet in diameter. This limb is thicker than the *trunk* of any non-sequoia tree in Yosemite's Mariposa Grove.

The Grizzly Giant stands 209 feet tall. That's about the same height as a 20-story building. Its *lowest* limb is about 100 feet above the ground.

TREE-MENDOUS

Many people who visit Yosemite National Park spend all their time in Yosemite Valley. This isn't surprising: few places in the world offer such jaw-dropping scenery. But the valley is really just a small part of Yosemite. There is much more to the park.

For example, giant sequoia (sih-KWOI-uh) trees reach high into the sky in forests near the park's western and southern boundaries. Giant sequoias can grow taller than a football field and sometimes live for more than 3,000 years. The park protects them from loggers, who might cut them down for their sturdy wood. Around 500 giant sequoias grow in Mariposa Grove in the southern part of Yosemite National Park. One of the most famous of these trees is called the Grizzly Giant, shown on the left. Read the captions to learn more about this amazing tree.

If you travel north of the valley, up in the high country of the Sierra Nevada, you'll find the Tuolumne (too-AH-luh-mee) River and its surrounding meadows. Hikers come here to enjoy miles of trails through a wilderness dotted with sparkling lakes. Black bears fish on the banks of the river as it flows peacefully through mountain-ringed meadows. Mule deer graze on the thick meadow grass and colorful wildflowers. Because this high mountain habitat is within the park, wildlife lives safely here. No one will hunt them or crowd them out by building homes on this land.

At the base of its trunk, the incredible Grizzly Giant measures more than 90 feet in circumference. To get an idea of how big this is, ask about 20 friends to form a circle with their arms outstretched and fingertips touching.

20 Friends

Check In Describe some of Yosemite's different ecosystems.

GENRE Geography Tour

Read to find out about the geographic features of Yosemite.

3 Days in Yosemite

by Brett Gover

Welcome to Yosemite National Park! This park is one of the most popular in the national park system, and by the end of our three-day tour you will know why. It's also one of the nation's oldest national parks. Many people know about Yosemite Valley with its super-high waterfalls, rock formations that look like giant domes, and cliffs that rise straight up for thousands of feet. But I think our towering mountains and humongous trees will amaze you, too. And just so you know, we won't just be seeing the sights from the comfort of a car. We'll be hiking, biking, and horseback riding, so get ready for a Yosemite adventure.

Most people visit the park to see the towering cliffs and high waterfalls of Yosemite Valley.

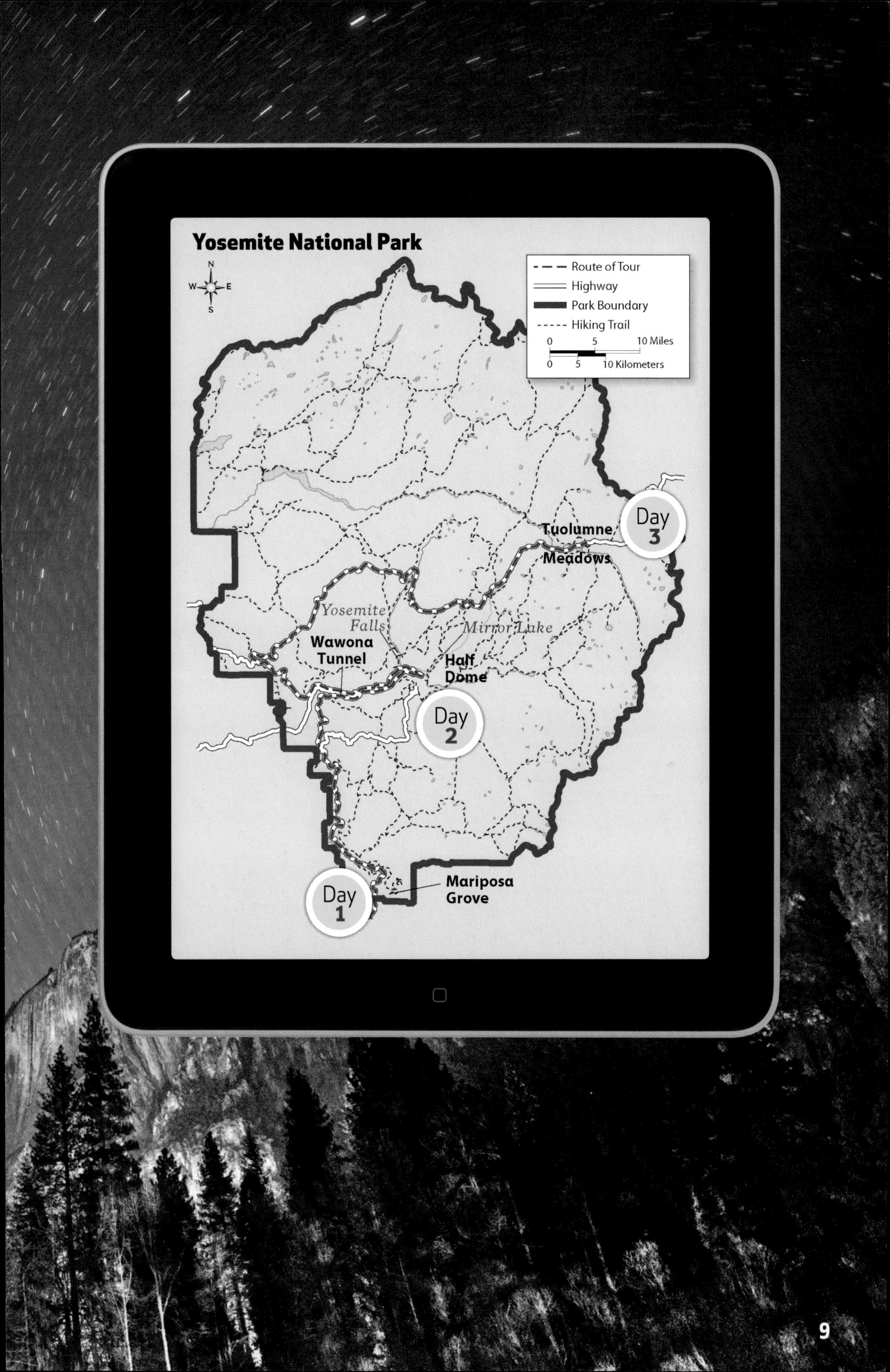
Yosemite National Park
N
W
E
S
Route of Tour
Highway
Park Boundary
Hiking Trail
0
5
10 Miles
0
5
10 Kilometers
Day 3
Tuolumne Meadows
Yosemite Falls
Mirror Lake
Wawona Tunnel
Half Dome
Day 2
Mariposa Grove
Day 1

A Grove of Giants

DAY 1

It's our first day in the park, and we're at our first stop, the Mariposa Grove. A **grove** is a group of trees, and the trees in this grove may surprise you. They are giant sequoias, and they are among the largest living things on Earth. They are not just incredibly tall—around 300 feet. They're also incredibly wide, reaching widths of 30 feet or more. Let's hike around the grove and see some of these leafy giants.

One of the first big trees we see is lying on its side. We call it the Fallen Monarch, and although it fell centuries ago, it has barely started to **decay**, or rot. Acid in the wood keeps the wood from breaking down and decaying quickly. Farther along the trail is one of the grove's biggest and oldest trees, the Grizzly Giant. It sprouted from a seed at least 1,800 years ago. Just beyond this enormous sequoia is the California Tunnel Tree. We can walk right through it!

Let's keep hiking along the trail to the Faithful Couple, two trees whose trunks have grown together. Higher up, they split apart again into two separate trees. At the highest part of the grove lies a fallen tree with a tunnel through it, the Wawona Tunnel Tree. After the tunnel was cut in 1881, millions of people passed through it, and the tree became famous. It would probably still be standing if a huge snowstorm hadn't piled a ton or more of snow on its highest branches in 1969, causing it to collapse.

Our last stop is the incredible Telescope Tree. Forest fires have hollowed the tree out completely, leaving only a sort of shell. When you stand inside and look up, you feel like you're looking through the world's biggest telescope. Surprisingly, this tree is still alive!

I hope you've enjoyed hiking among the graceful giants of Mariposa Grove. Tomorrow we'll head to Yosemite Valley.

California Tunnel Tree

Fallen Monarch

The Faithful Couple

Telescope Tree

Rock Walls and Waterfalls

DAY 2

Today we'll visit Yosemite Valley. Most visitors get their first look at Yosemite Valley from afar, as they drive from the Mariposa Grove north through the Wawona Tunnel. As they come out on the far side of the tunnel, the valley stretches out before them. To their left rises the huge rock called El Capitan, the largest single piece of granite in the world. To their right is Bridalveil Fall, a misty ribbon of water falling from a 620-foot-high cliff. Far in the distance is Half Dome, one of Yosemite's most famous rock formations. From this view, Half Dome really does look like a rounded dome that has been sliced in half.

One of the best ways to explore the valley is on two wheels, so we'll be hopping on rental bikes and setting off. A short distance from the lodge, we'll stop to check out Yosemite Falls, the highest waterfall in North America. The water falls more than 2,400 feet from the rim of the valley to the Merced River in three dramatic drops. The first drop is nearly 200 feet taller than New York City's Empire State Building, and the third drop is taller than the Statue of Liberty! You can hike to the top, but the trail is very steep.

Our next destination is Mirror Lake, near the eastern end of the valley. This small lake—really more of a pond—is called Mirror Lake because the valley walls are reflected in its smooth water. Mirror Lake is famous for its crystal-clear reflection of Half Dome.

Let's take time to ride through the valley and back to the lodge, crossing and recrossing the bends of the Merced River. Tomorrow we'll head for the high country.

Snow melts each spring high in the Sierra Nevada. It feeds Yosemite Creek, which plunges into the valley as Yosemite Falls. That's why the falls are most powerful in late spring.

The High Sierra

DAY 3

Today is the last day of our tour of Yosemite National Park, and we will spend it riding horses in the Sierra Nevada—the high mountains of eastern California. By the time we reach Tuolumne Meadows, we'll be nearly a mile higher than we were in Yosemite Valley. That's why they call it the high country!

Here in the meadows, the Tuolumne River and other streams flow in a winding course across a level area of land that is covered with tall grass and colorful wildflowers. Where the land begins to rise at the edges of the meadows, forests take over. All around us, rugged mountain peaks rise far above the forests. Some peaks are still capped with snow from last winter.

Now let's saddle up at the Tuolumne Meadows Stable and set out on a trail that curves around a tall rock dome and then follows the Tuolumne River upstream. Where the river splits, the trail follows a narrow **branch** called the Lyell Fork. We're riding through the rugged mountains to Twin Bridges, where two short wooden bridges cross the stream in a high mountain meadow. Let's dismount from our horses and wade in the cold, shallow waters. We'll spend the next couple of hours exploring, picnicking, and relaxing on the stream's smooth granite bank. Then we'll get back on our horses and return to the stable.

I hope you enjoyed our three days in Yosemite. Although you've seen Yosemite's three main regions and many of its unique features, our park has so much more to offer—more than most people could discover in a lifetime. So come back anytime. Yosemite's a great place to explore!

An amazing view rewards hikers who reach Tenaya Peak in Yosemite's high country.

Check In Which part of Yosemite National Park would you most like to explore? Describe it.

GENRE Legend **Read to find out** how one legend says El Capitan was formed.

The Legend of EL CAPITAN

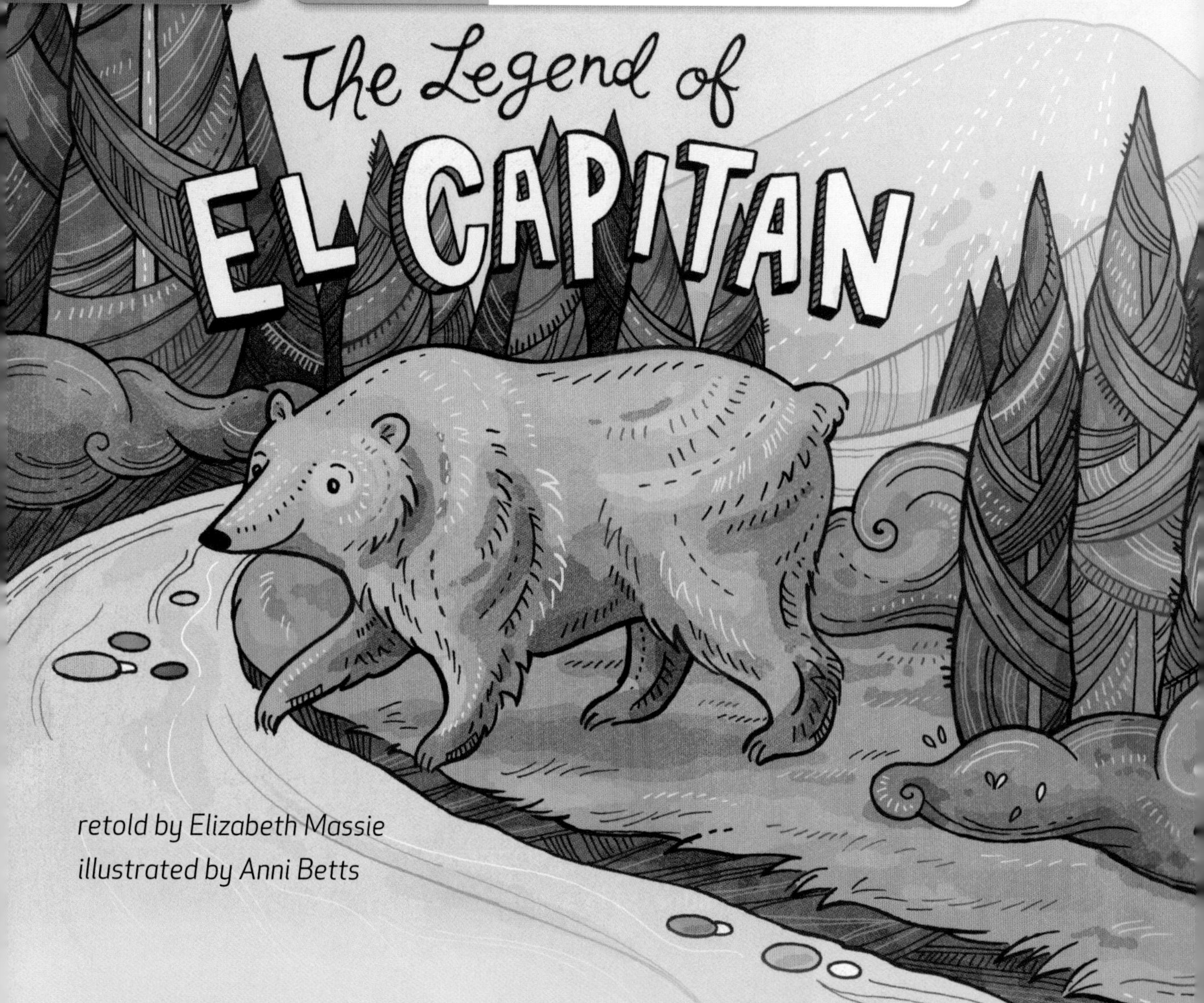

retold by Elizabeth Massie
illustrated by Anni Betts

Hundreds of years ago, Native Americans called the Miwok settled along creeks and rivers in what is now Yosemite National Park. They hunted, fished, and traded with neighboring tribes. Like other tribes, they told legends, or stories to explain the natural world around them. One awesome natural formation in Yosemite Valley is a gigantic granite column, the largest of its type in the world. This column, called El Capitan, has become a favorite destination of rock climbers. The Miwok called it To-to-kon-oo-lah, and they explained its existence with a legend, retold here.

One cool autumn morning, Mother Grizzly took her two cubs to the bank of the Merced River so she could check the fish traps she had placed there the day before.

"Stay here and don't go running off," said Mother Grizzly to the cubs. "I must go up and down the river to see if I've caught any trout and pikeminnow. I don't want to have to come looking for you when I return."

"Oh, Mother," Little Cub replied with a roll of his little brown eyes. "You know we always do what we're supposed to do."

"We promise we'll stay put and won't get into any trouble," said Small Cub with a nod of her small brown head.

Mother Grizzly kissed each cub in turn and then ambled off down the riverbank to check her traps.

While Mother Grizzly was gone, Little Cub and Small Cub had a grand time playing tag, chasing butterflies, and wading in the cool, shallow water at the river's edge.

Finally, as the sun smiled down on them from the highest point in the sky, the cubs fell asleep, exhausted, on top of a large, flat rock. As they slept, the rock started to rattle and rumble and shake. Then it began to grow, rising up so high it nearly touched the clouds.

In mid-afternoon, Mother Grizzly returned with a sack full of trout and pikeminnow from her traps. She looked here and there but couldn't find her cubs anywhere. Hurling the sack of fish aside, she threw back her head and roared at the top of her lungs, "Someone please help me find my missing children!"

Many animals rushed to the riverside to assist Mother Grizzly, who stood weeping with her face in her paws. Deer Mouse came, as did Black Rat, Gray Fox, Bobcat, Mountain Lion, and a tiny inchworm. They comforted Mother Grizzly. They told her to be brave—they would do all they could to find the missing cubs.

Crane, who had been circling overhead, swooped down and asked, "Do you see that tall stone mountain that reaches the sky, Mother Grizzly? As I flew past it, I saw two cubs sleeping soundly on top of it."

Mother Grizzly was terrified that her cubs would awaken, become frightened, and perhaps tumble from that dizzying height. Mountain Lion reassured her, saying, “Don’t fear, Mother Grizzly. We’ll get your children down to safety.”

“Yes,” said Gray Fox, “we will do all we can to …” And then she stopped and started to laugh, for she had seen the little inchworm, whose name was To-to-kon-oo-lah, standing among the animals.

“To-to-kon-oo-lah,” said Gray Fox with a chuckle, “there is no need for you to be here. You are much too small to help.”

“Go on about your business, To-to-kon-oo-lah,” said Deer Mouse and Bobcat. “We’ll rescue the bear cubs from the tall mountaintop.”

Deer Mouse was first to try to get to the top of the great mountain, leaping as high as she could but reaching only two feet before falling back down. Her tiny claws left little marks on the side of the mountain.

Next came Black Rat, who leapt up but reached only three feet before sliding back down again, leaving his claw marks on the side of the mountain as well.

"Step out of my way," said Gray Fox as she moved to the base of the mountain and flexed her paws. She hunched down, wriggled her bushy tail, and then jumped with all her might. Yet she was only able to leap ten feet up the mountainside before she, too, slid back down, creating even more claw marks in the stone.

"Oh!" wailed Mother Grizzly. "I fear no one will be able to rescue my poor cubs!"

"Now, friends," said Bobcat with a shake of his head, "just stand back and watch how it's done." He drew a deep breath and then jumped high, his paws out and his claws extended. He reached a fine height of 15 feet, but of course, that was not high enough. He slid back down, his claws scraping the stone with a loud, squealing sound.

Mountain Lion, the most powerful of them all, seemed to be the only hope left. She nodded at Mother Grizzly, then narrowed her eyes, tightened her muscles, and sprang up against the mountain with a grunt and a growl. She reached a great height of 20 feet, scrabbled with her claws to get higher, but only slid back down like the others.

"There is no hope, no hope at all," sobbed Mother Grizzly as the animals gathered around her once more. "My children may never be returned to me!"

Then Bobcat looked up and exclaimed, "Look over there! To-to-kon-oo-lah is climbing the mountain!"

And so To-to-kon-oo-lah was, creeping ever so slowly up the steep, rocky surface with his sticky little feet. The animals watched in amazement as he moved inch by inch, his face set with determination.

They watched for a day, then a week, and then a month. Up, up, the inchworm climbed, many thousands of feet toward the top of the mountain. Autumn ended and winter came with snow and winds, but the little inchworm did not stop or turn back. He pressed onward until, as the last storm of winter was over, he had reached the top.

To-to-kon-oo-lah smiled at the sleeping cubs and then he tapped each one very gently with his foot.

"Wake up, Little Cub and Small Cub," he said. "Your mother wants you back home again."

The cubs rubbed their eyes and slowly sat up. Then their eyes flew open as they saw where they were.

"Oh, we will never get down safely!" cried Little Cub.

"I will help you," said To-to-kon-oo-lah.

"But I'm afraid of heights! What if we fall?" wailed Small Cub.

"I had time to study the mountain on my way up," said To-to-kon-oo-lah, "and I know where there are footholds to help you."

And so To-to-kon-oo-lah helped the cubs climb back down to the valley floor, where they were reunited with Mother Grizzly.

The other animals named the mountain "To-to-kon-oo-lah" in honor of the brave and determined inchworm. Today, most people call it "El Capitan." And to this day, some of the animals' claw marks can still be seen on its tall, granite sides.

Check In What did the legend of the animals teach you about the shape of El Capitan?

GENRE Reference Article | **Read to find out** about extreme rock climbing in Yosemite.

SUPER Climbers

by Grace Coffey

Dean Potter clings to Glacier Point in Yosemite National Park.

Imagine clinging to a cliff 3,000 feet above the ground with only the strength of your fingers and toes to keep you from falling. No safety equipment. No ropes. Just you and the cliff. That's what some super climbers do. Rock climbing is an extreme sport that involves skill, risk, and a thirst for adventure. The soaring rocks and steep cliffs of Yosemite attract climbers from all over the world, but very few take the risks that make them super climbers. A super climber is a rock climber who tackles extremely risky climbs in the most challenging climbing locations. Once super climbers have scouted a route, they scale it quickly, with little or no equipment. But super climbers train for years before tackling climbs like these, so don't try this at home!

Climber:

DEAN POTTER

Record-breaking super climber Dean Potter considers Yosemite his home base. He can **ascend**, or climb up, some of Yosemite's granite cliffs faster than the time it takes to watch a movie.

Climbing Style:

FREE SOLO

Potter uses a dangerous style of climbing called free solo. He climbs with no ropes or safety equipment. Without supplies or gear to haul, he only needs to pull up the weight of his body.

Location:

GLACIER POINT

Potter free solos to a popular lookout area called Glacier Point, 3,214 feet above the ground. Glacier Point offers outstanding views of Yosemite. This is one of the toughest free climbs in the park.

^ Half Dome is another tempting challenge for super climbers. Long ago, a river of ice, or glacier, moved through Yosemite Valley, cutting off part of Half Dome. Today, this peak has a rounded slope on one side and a sharp cliff on the other side.

A View Like No Other

Until climbers first conquered it in 1958, the peak called El Capitan was considered impossible to climb. The first climb took 47 days. Even today, most climbers take four to five days to reach the top. Speedy super climbers have cut the record down to less than two-and-a-half hours.

"The Nose" is the most famous climbing route up El Capitan. This challenging route goes almost straight up the huge rock. It takes an average climber several days to reach the top, but **descending**, or going down, is much easier. That only takes about four hours.

^ **El Capitan**

> **Kevin Jorgenson scales El Capitan in Yosemite National Park.**

Climber:

KEVIN JORGESON

Kevin Jorgeson got his first taste of climbing at a gym when he was 12 years old. This California-born climbing enthusiast found rock climbing to be a natural and comfortable sport. As a teenager, he began winning national climbing competitions. He even traveled to Europe to compete on the high mountains there.

Climbing Style:

FREE CLIMBING

Like many other super climbers, Jorgeson free climbs using pitons, ropes, and carabiners. Pitons are metal spikes that fasten a climber's ropes to the rock. Carabiners are oblong-shaped metal loops that are attached to the ropes. A carabiner on Jorgeson's climbing rope attaches to his harness. These climbing tools keep him safely secured to the rock wall in case he slips and falls. That's pretty much his only gear.

Location:

EL CAPITAN

This single, massive rock is the world's largest granite **monolith**. El Capitan is the most tempting challenge of Yosemite to avid climbers. The "captain" or "chief" is one of the ultimate challenges of rock climbing. Its walls rise more than 3,000 feet from the floor of Yosemite Valley. Those who have reached the top say the spectacular view is worth the extreme effort.

What Goes Up Must Come Down

Super climbers can also be super jumpers. After a challenging climb to the top of a peak like Half Dome, some super climbers opt to **BASE jump** instead of hiking back down. BASE jumpers wear parachutes or special "wingsuits" that fill with air when they leap. They glide for a bit and then open their parachutes (or spread their "wings") to land safely.

These BASE jumpers are leaping off the summit of Half Dome. They will land on the floor of Yosemite Valley, nearly 5,000 feet below.

Descent Style:
BASE JUMPING

Are these super climbers really parachuting off a cliff in Yosemite? Yes! They're BASE jumping. BASE jumpers launch themselves from some crazy places, including cliffs, bridges, and the summit, or top, of Half Dome in Yosemite. After climbing Half Dome, they depend on lightweight parachutes to float safely back down to the valley floor.

Location:
HALF DOME

Half Dome attracts many thrill seekers. The hiking trail to the top of the rock is hard enough. Hikers must use steel cables attached to the steep, rounded side of the rock to reach the very top. Only the most expert climbers scale Half Dome's cliff face, or side. The cliff is 2,000 feet straight up. And only the most extreme super climbers tackle the challenge with no equipment except the parachute they hope will deliver them safely back to the foot of Half Dome.

What does BASE mean?

It represents four different types of structures that the jumpers leap from.

B UILDINGS
A NTENNAS
S PANS (BRIDGES)
E ARTH

Focusing a camera on other climbers while balancing on the side of a cliff yourself is no easy task, but that's how *National Geographic* photographer Jimmy Chin earns a living. With dangling equipment and nerves of steel, Chin climbs alongside his subjects to capture the best photographs. He shoots about three or four major expeditions each year, documenting death-defying trips on mountains all over the world and relying heavily on his experience as a climber and skier. Check out Chin's photos below. It's no wonder he's considered one of the top extreme mountain photographers in the world!

Hanging By a Thread

To capture these images, Chin relies upon his advanced climbing skills and extreme bravery. Jimmy loves free climbing, but sometimes this is not an option when his eyes are focused on the athlete and his hands are wrapped around a camera. Chin often needs to opt for aid climbing, which uses ropes, carabiners, hammers, pulleys, and other safety equipment. On long climbs, they even sleep in special tents called portaledges they can secure to the rock. No matter what safety equipment they use, rock climbers must be well trained.

Chin uses a rope, harness, and carabiners to make his way up El Capitan.

Check In Why are these adventurers called "super climbers"?

Discuss

1. Tell about some of the ways you think the four selections in this book are linked.

2. Discuss the history of the park and tell what people have done and continue to do to protect the park's habitats and ecosystems.

3. The first and the second selections both describe the geography and sights of Yosemite National Park. Describe how some of the park's natural features were formed and continue to form.

4. What makes a super climber different from a regular rock climber? What do you think about the risks super climbers take?

5. What do you still want to know about the wonders of Yosemite National Park and why people try to keep this special place safe?